A
Little Ins

Jasmine Birtles

B■XTREE

First published 2000 by Boxtree
an imprint of Macmillan Publishers Ltd 25 Eccleston Place London SW1W 9NF
Basingstoke and Oxford

www.macmillan.co.uk

Associated companies throughout the world

ISBN 0 7522 7146 6

1 3 5 7 9 8 6 4 2

A CIP catalogue record for this book is available from the British Library.

Designed by Nigel Davies
Printed by Redwood Books, Trowbridge, Wiltshire

SISTERS

As a long-suffering sister you'll know that little brothers are a walking advert for vasectomies. And a little sister can only be relied upon to photocopy your diary and pin it up around the school for everyone to laugh at (unless she's dyslexic, in which case she'll just try to read your dairy). Still, at least you don't have to waste energy putting yourself down. That's what all your siblings are there for. So, if you want to keep your sanity at home – and at school – pick up some top tips from this book. And remember, killing your brother may be fratricide but if he's a pest, it's just pesticide.

5

There's only one thing worse
than your little sister
wanting to borrow your clothes:
her not wanting to borrow them …

… or your brother
wanting to borrow them.

Be tactful about your sister.
She's not an 'airhead',
she's 'reality impaired'.

Be tactful about your brother.
He's not 'pissed as a fart',
he has become 'accidentally horizontal'.

'Sisters, sisters,
there were never such devoted sisters',
as ...
those who share everything
– like measles, mumps and head lice.

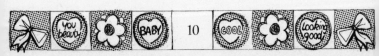

A sister is someone
who is happy to listen to your problems
– then laughs about them afterwards
as she points you out
to all her friends.

Teenage brothers:
a walking advertisement for vasectomies.

Younger brothers can grow on you,
but then so do warts.

The best way to keep your youth
is not to introduce him to your big sister.

Older sisters –
a mobile wardrobe and make-up unit.

When your brother goes to college
you can tell yourself
you're not losing a companion,
you're gaining a TV and
some soiled pornographic magazines.

Stepmothers are like scratch cards
– rub them enough and they'll produce money.

Sisters are doing it for themselves, but only if
they can't get Dad to do it for them.

The worst thing about being the youngest
in the family is all the hand-me-downs –
especially if you're an only child.

It's better to be the younger sister.
You get to be just as naughty but sooner.

To err is human;
to forgive is not in your sisters' genetic make-up.

Tattoo your address on your
little brother's forehead. That way if
he gets lost he can post himself home.

Use younger brothers
and sisters as a personal slave
– to fetch things,
make you a cup of tea,
and milk the asses for your bath.

Take a photo of your
younger brother in girl's clothes.
You never know when you'll need
to blackmail him, like when he brings home
his first girlfriend.

Did you hear about the dyslexic girl
who read her sister's dairy?

Older brothers should stand up for you,
not on you.

If a cute guy asks 'Are you sisters?', beware.
If you say yes, he might add, 'See you left
Cinderella at home, then.'

Do not read your sister's diary in secret.
Photocopy it and pin it up around the school.

Don't barge into your sister's bedroom
without knocking.
It can be annoying, especially if you were
separated at birth and she always believed
you died in a freak yachting accident
fifteen years ago.

What's the worst side of having a brother?
Fratri-cide.

The Russian for brother is 'brat'.
That figures.

Brothers are like badgers.
It's illegal to gas them or dig them out
with pit bull terriers.

If your dad has a daughter by a previous
marriage she's your half-sister. Does that make
his cat by a previous marriage your half-cat?

If Barbie is so popular,
why do you have to buy all her friends?

How can you tell if your sister has been
using your make-up? It looks like a clown's
convention was held in your bedroom.

A few kind words never hurt anyone.
Try using a sharpened tent peg.

Start a nasty rumour at school
about your sister and see if you recognize it
when it gets back to you.

Blood is thicker than water?
Hey, mayonnaise is thicker than water.

To err is human, to forgive divine. Ha!
Double chocolate gateau is divine.
Forgiveness is just so-so.

Famous Sisters:
The Corrs, Sister Sledge,
The Andrews Sisters,
The Beverley Sisters,
Seven Sisters,
Shakespear's Sister,
The North Hackney and Haringey Lesbian
Feminist Collective Drop-In Centre Sisters.

Less famous sisters:
Sharon Queen of Scots,
Tricia Navratilova,
Beverley of Arc,
and
the Virgin Maureen.

Separated at birth:
Anthea
and Tina Turner,
Pamela
and Moira Anderson,
Ulrika
and Amy Johnson.

Envying your little sister
is like a blunt pencil – they're both pointless.

Play doctors and nurses –
don't sleep for thirty-six hours,
drink too much and go round the house
mopping up sick.

   31

Ballet
– the last chance you'll get to stand
half-naked with your legs apart,
showing your knickers,
and not be described as 'asking for it'.

Brothers don't like listening to your problems.
It takes their minds off themselves.

If your mum is angry,
don't let her brush your hair.

If you want a kitten,
start out by asking for a pony.

If you want a pony, ask for a pony.
In your sweetest voice.
Four thousand times.

Felt tips are not good substitutes
for lipstick
- or eyeshadow.

Being a girl is great because we can be groupies.
Boy groupies are called stalkers.

Laugh and the world laughs with you.
Cry and you'll probably win the argument.

It is unladylike to fight with your sisters –
unless they are smaller and weaker than you
are and unlikely to snitch.

Don't let your brother become paranoid.
Tell him he really is unpopular.

Lose several pounds of unsightly fat.
Leave your little brother at
the shopping centre.

Tell your brother he's not as clever
as he thinks he is.
No one could be that clever.

When you look at your brother,
remember it could be worse.
You could have been a twin.

Beauty is only skin deep,
so try not to scratch.

If your brother is worried about
not being able to dance, reassure him
that those people pointing and laughing
are really trying to encourage him.

Think of your brother as a little jewel,
buried in the dirt.

You are what you eat
but don't let your life go down the toilet.

Tell your brother's girlfriend not to worry,
that none of the rumours are true.
Then refuse to discuss the rumours.

Sister Sledge is a pop group
– not a winter sport.

Don't put yourself down.
That's what brothers are for.

If your brother insists you should iron his
clothes, then do it while he's wearing them.

Blood is thicker than water:
brothers are thicker
than any known substance.

Worry your brother by referring
to his room as the 'guest room'.

    43

Being true to yourself shouldn't mean
being false to everyone else.

The family gives you a start in life
but don't let it finish you off.

    44

Always ask your brother's advice
so you'll know exactly what not to do.

Wear sensible shoes:
one left-footed and one right-footed.

Accidents will happen.
Just look at your brother.

Look on the bright side.
Someone will marry your brother,
so there'll always be someone worse off
than yourself.

 46

Boys will be game boys.
Pity you can't take their batteries out.

Help Mum around the house.
Buy her rollerblades so that
she can do it all faster.

If you learn to drive, drive fast.
Get home before the accidents happen.

It's time to worry when your dolls
are dressed like a princess
and you look like the ugly sister.

Sticking voodoo pins in your Barbie
is healthy. Sticking them in Claudia Schiffer
is an arrestable offence.

Always say the three little words to your sister:
'We're not related.'

49

Boys are like computers.
They store a lot of facts
but basically they're clueless.

The last thing you should do is ruin
your brother's self-confidence. So leave that
to the end of the argument.

As you get older you'll find
you get tense at a certain time of the month
– the time when you have to pay off
the interest on your credit cards.

Sibling rivalry
– seeing who can lisp the longest.

Face it,
a new eyeshadow won't make you
look like a supermodel,
earn you millions
and turn your life around.
A new lipstick, on the other hand …

Boys are like a good wine.
They should be stamped on
and kept in the dark
until they mature into something
you'd like to have at dinner.

Books your parents won't buy you:
The Barbie Twins and the Vice Squad,
The Gary Glitter Bumper Book of Facts,
and
Controlling the Staffroom
– Accusations that Always Get Attention.

 54

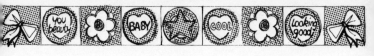

Don't ask your boyfriend
what he's thinking about
unless you enjoy discussing
pocket fluff or whether Lara Croft
is one cool pixelated bitch.

Don't do a Cosmo quiz with your boyfriend.
His idea of multiple choice is
those models in the fashion pages.

90% of the hunkiest men in the world have
intellects rivalled by gardening tools.

Baby brothers
– experiments in Artificial Stupidity.

If at first you don't succeed, bat your eyelids,
look all girlie and get the nearest man
to do it for you.

Put-downs for flashers:
'I've seen better on a Christmas tree,'
'Yes, it looks like a willy but smaller'
and
'No thanks, I've already eaten.'

Spice Girl vacancies still available:
Scowling Spice,
Sexually-Indeterminate Spice,
Sugary Spice,
Septic-Tongued Spice
and Ex-Slapper Spice?

It's not possible to live like
the characters in Friends
and still have friends.

Beauty is only skin deep but
alimony can last a lifetime.

Love is the most important thing
in the world but cashmere
comes a close second.

Don't rush into falling in love
– take your time, enjoy the pain.

How to kiss with confidence:
never eat spinach.

How to tell your boyfriend's got taste:
hey, he's going out with you, isn't he?

Never move quickly except to avoid work
or track down a good excuse.

If at first you don't succeed, there's always
next year/decade/reincarnation.

When your brother says,
'That's a girl's job,' what he really means is that
it's difficult, smelly and thankless.

No one is completely useless.
It could be that your brother's real purpose
in life is to serve as a warning to others.

It's better to have beauty rather
than brains because the average man can see
better than he can think.

Names that could get you shunned
in the playground:
Hildegard, Ethel, Hyacinth, Vanessa Feltz.

Average teenage girl's Saturday night:
five hours getting washed,
doing make-up, hair and choosing
the right clothes to 'drive him wild'
as advised in magazines;
three hours hanging outside the chip shop
with girlfriends;
going home alone.

You know you have a
dysfunctional family if the bikers
next door complain about the noise,
your baby sister is named after
a famous serial killer and
holidays are celebrated by
sniffing glue and kicking a toaster
round the house.

Your mum's got problems if you
have to buy separate Mother's Day cards
for her personalities.

If you share a bunk bed, make sure the
bed-wetter sleeps on the bottom bunk.

Put into practice the honesty,
openness and sense of justice
your parents instilled in you
by shopping them and their
'exotic pot plants'
to the police.

Ruin your parents' Sundays.
Insist on going to Sunday school
instead of accompanying them
to their place of worship
– the garden centre.

Ask for the strength
to change the things you can
and the grace to accept
the things you can't.
Oh, and a big bag of money.

The correct three genie wishes.

1) Your sister dead.

2) Eternal beauty, fame and money.

3) Your sister dead again, just to make sure.

Phrases to get your stepfather into trouble:

'He said it was just our little secret,'

'He said if I told anyone
he'd have to go away for a very long time,'

'Let me draw it for you.'

You know your sister's two-timing
if she buys her Valentine's cards
in packs of ten.

You know your sister's cheating
if she CCs her Valentine's cards.

Never underestimate the pulling power
of a school uniform – or the perviness
of the guys you'll pull.

How come no one's got a food allergy
to foie gras, filet mignon or Chardonnay?

Love can make you moon around –
fine so long as you don't
do it out of the back of the school bus.

Refuse to be a bridesmaid. Unless you enjoy
looking like a toilet roll cosy.

Favourite colours for bridesmaids' outfits:
peach, apricot and peachy-apricot.

Date movie?
Choose a really scary one.
More chances to cuddle up to him.

Families are like fudge –
sweet but there are often hidden nuts.

'Ow' –
the first word a baby learns
if he has older siblings.

'Show off' –
a best friend who is more talented
than you.

Home is where
the pocket money is.

If you complain a lot you get
to live longer. Start now.

Try to remember what you know
while you're young. This is the only time
in your life you'll know everything.

Anyone can be a model –
for Airfix.

Learn to drive early.
Two in the morning.
There's a lot less traffic around.

Try crazy golf.
Go to a normal course, but play insanely
while screeching on about
that damn windmill.

Don't wait to join Club 18–30.
Join something with a higher IQ right now.

82

You're on a diet when …
you order double sausage and chips,
Black Forest gateau and a Diet Coke.

Exercise every day.
You'll die healthier.

Seminars for brothers:
'The remote control – overcoming
dependency',
'Your bicycle – why it isn't a Ducati 916'
and
'Change your underwear – change your life'.

    84

Don't brush
before visiting the dentist.
Munch a Mars bar
in the waiting room.
Let him work for his money.

You have nothing to fear except fear itself –
unless you have a brother.

Thirteen is an unlucky number –
if it's your bust measurement.

Beauty
is an inside job.

Never steal your sister's boyfriend;
he has no taste in women.

Learn as many languages as possible.
One of them might enable you
to talk to your parents.

Don't bother eating chocolate.
Just apply it directly to your hips.

If you can put your trousers on
over your head, you're too thin.

If Mum and Dad are your best friends –
try and get out more often.

Your family can be relied upon
for one thing only –
birthday cards.

Don't believe what they say in the magazines.
The sleek do not inherit the earth.

If your parents force you
to help with the gardening, trim the hedge
so it spells the word HELP!

Dating a boy your own age is simple;
an older man may need carbon-dating.

What goes up must come down
but if alcohol is involved, what goes down
may well come up!

Don't explain yourself.
Your friends accept you as you are and
your enemies don't care anyway.

Definition of a diet:
a short period of starvation followed by a
rapid gain of twelve pounds.

Consider what a nightmare it would be
if all your daydreams
came true.

When people ask how you are,
they don't really want you to tell them.

If your parents don't like you
watching much television,
rent some videos instead.

    94

Acne –
nature's way of protecting you from men
before you're old enough to control them.

Whatever the problem,
the answer is shopping.

Running away from home
won't help –
unless you're desperate for fame
and being on missing person's
posters will do.

Who you want:
Robbie Williams.

Who you get:
Kenneth Williams.

Inform your little brother
that there is no Tooth Fairy
and there is no Santa Claus
but the scary monster
that lives under his bed
is very, very real.

If you're good at hair-pulling,
half-Nelsons and slam-dunking,
you're either a female wrestler –
or an elder sister whose make-up
just got 'borrowed'.

Worry your parents.
Ask them if they like the idea of
grandchildren.

Always let your sister have the last word,
as long as the last word is 'Ouch!'

Don't flatter to deceive.
Leave that to your boyfriend.

Go on a blind date.
Poke him in the eyes when he arrives.

 103

Be careful if you're led to the altar.
Who will be making the sacrifice?

If at first you don't succeed,
destroy all evidence that you tried.

Just when you get your room how you like it
your mum will make you tidy it up.

Rule of dating:
you will take two hours getting ready
and he will be two hours late.

Boy Bands.
So called because it's not immediately obvious
what their gender is.

Eat, drink and be merry,
so long as you don't mind being a silly,
overweight alcoholic.

There's nothing so traitorous
as bathroom scales you can't adjust.

Never go out with a guy who has
better hair than you.

Buy your older sister chocolate.
Let her try out the bad skin
and ferocious acne before you.

Little girls are made of Sugar and Spice –
no, that's Christmas puddings.

Boyfriend lies #1.
'Your sister's young, thin
and blonde?
Of course I don't
fancy her.'

Buy your sister a really nice
birthday gift –
then watch her go crazy
trying to guess which of her things
your broke.

Feminists say that all women
are sisters:
OK, so that's pathologically jealous,
competitive and
passive-aggressive.

If your boyfriend asks
if you and your sister
ever get naked together,
tell him, 'Yeah, all the time -
when we were three!'

Younger sisters are just
stunt-girls for new hairstyles, make-up
and dangerous fashion decisions.

Freak out your twin sister at the disco
by jabbing yourself in the leg with a fork.
Just watch her dance.

A sister is like a computer.
Easy to use and you can boot her up every day.

If you want to get out of family meals,
ask about the facts of life
every time you sit down.

How to diet:
watch your little brother
eat his dinner without the aid of
serviettes, cutlery or
any sense of facial geography.

Never take fashion tips from your mum –
unless she's just opened an account for you
at Harvey Nichols.

If you get terrible marks at school,
console your parents with the thought
that at least you weren't cheating.

If you want to inherit,
be helpful to all your relatives. You won't
be in the will unless you show willing.

If you're having difficulty opening
a tight bottle of nail varnish just tell your
little brother not to touch it.

When it comes to boyfriends
be like your cat –
stay aloof, only allow yourself to be petted
when you feel like it
and occasionally dig your claws
in his flesh to show how
much you really like him.

Monday morning affirmations:
'I have a great body ...
well, it's better than my sister's,'
'I'm cleverer than my brother ...
of course anyone is cleverer than him
but that's not the point ...'
and
'I'm really good at watching TV.'

If you sneak on your brother or sister
try to sound reluctant about it.
Phrases like 'I'm only telling you this
because I'm worried about him,'
or 'Now do you agree that she should
be put in a home?'
always go down well.

Acceptable accessories
when fighting with siblings:
tickling stick, water pistol, wet flannel,
your dad.
Unacceptable accessories:
Smith and Weston .45, knuckle duster,
Lennox Lewis.

Help your brothers and sisters'
immune systems –
offer to cook for them.

If your parents are trying to be 'cool',
snap them out of it.
Tell them you're gay.

The average brother is to tact
and sensitivity what Frank Bruno
is to ballet.

Killing your brother is fratricide,
but if he's a pest,
that's only pesticide.

Try and develop periods
every fortnight.
You'll never have to do games
and you can kill your brother
and never go to prison for it.

Don't bother looking for blemishes
in the morning. Your brother will always
keep you informed of any new ones.

If you're creative you can look great
in second-hand things …
unless it's your sister's old boyfriend.

When in doubt, tell the truth.
When in deep doo-doo, tell on your brother.

Toys they'll never buy you:
My Little Pregnancy Kit,
Home Torture Set,
Dominatrix Barbie.

The answers to life's problems
are not in a boyfriend –
they're in your make-up bag!

Teenage girls are hormones with hair.
Teenage boys are just hormones.
See, you are better than them.

When they made Jasmine they broke the mould –
but some of it grew back. She is currently in training for
'Most Annoying Woman in Great Britain' and is widely
tipped to win. She is so irritating she was once beaten
up by Mother Theresa – and Gandhi. She likes to make
an exhibition of herself and was once arrested naked at
the Tate. She is very musical and on long winter
evenings likes to sit at home, humming an old Celtic
tune and accompanying herself on a lute – not the
musical instrument but that free ads paper everyone
likes. She is eighty-three and once snogged Chris Evans.